FINGERPICKING ACOUSTIC

T0055449

ISBN 978-0-634-06537-8

For all works contained herein:
Unauthorized copying, arranging, adapting, recording
or public performance is an infringement of copyright.
Infringers are liable under the law.

Visit Hal Leonard Online at www.halleonard.com

HAL•LEONARD®
CORPORATION
7777 W. BLUEMOUND RD. P.O. BOX 13819 MILWAUKEE, WI 53213

INTRODUCTION TO FINGERSTYLE GUITAR

Fingerstyle (a.k.a. fingerpicking) is a guitar technique that means you literally pick the strings with your right-hand fingers and thumb. This contrasts with the conventional technique of strumming and playing single notes with a pick (a.k.a. flatpicking). For fingerpicking, you can use any type of guitar: acoustic steel-string, nylon-string classical, or electric.

THE RIGHT HAND

The most common right-hand position is shown here.

Use a high wrist; arch your palm as if you were holding a ping-pong ball. Keep the thumb outside and away from the fingers, and let the fingers do the work rather than lifting your whole hand.

The thumb generally plucks the bottom strings with downstrokes on the left side of the thumb and thumbnail. The other fingers pluck the higher strings using upstokes with the fleshy tip of the fingers and fingernails. The thumb and fingers should pluck one string per stroke and not brush over several strings.

Another picking option you may choose to use is called hybrid picking (a.k.a. plectrum-style fingerpicking). Here, the pick is usually held between the thumb and first finger, and the three remaining fingers are assigned to pluck the higher strings.

THE LEFT HAND

The left-hand fingers are numbered 1 though 4.

Be sure to keep your fingers arched, with each joint bent; if they flatten out across the strings, they will deaden the sound when you fingerpick. As a general rule, let the strings ring as long as possible when playing fingerstyle.

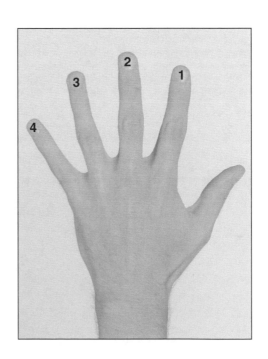

Blowin' in the Wind

Words and Music by Bob Dylan

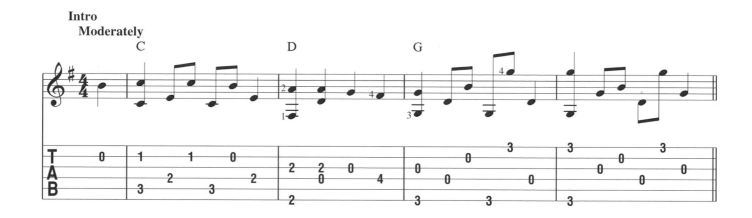

1. How man - y roads must _ a man walk _ down _ be - fore _ you

2., 3. *See additional lyrics*

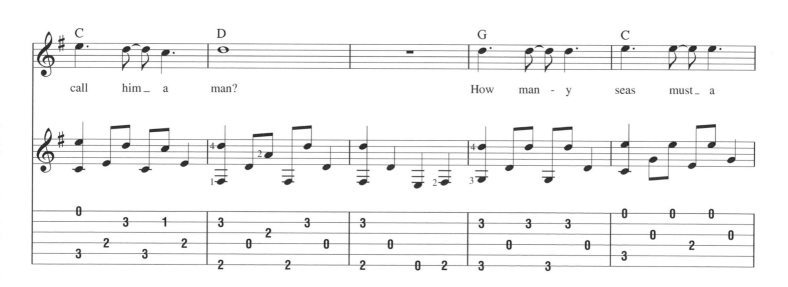

call him _ a man? How man - y seas must _ a

Copyright © 1962 Warner Bros. Inc.
Copyright Renewed 1990 Special Rider Music
International Copyright Secured   All Rights Reserved
Reprinted by Permission of Music Sales Corporation

white dove ___ sail ___ be - fore ___ she sleeps in ___ the sand?

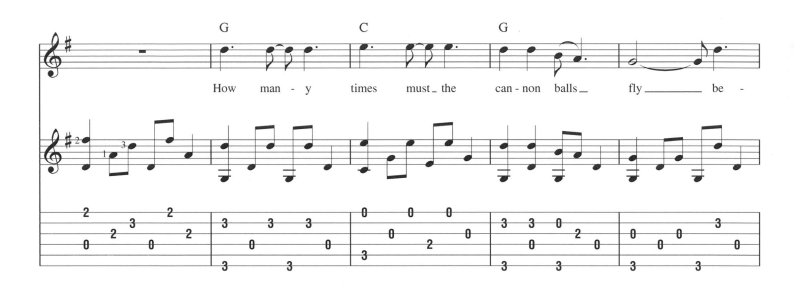

How man - y times must ___ the can-non balls ___ fly ___ be -

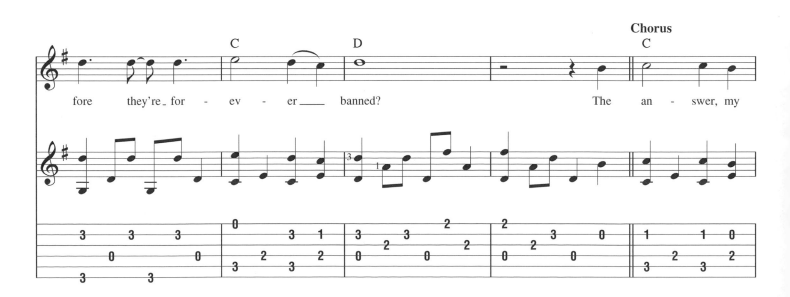

fore they're _ for - ev - er ___ banned? The an - swer, my

Chorus

Additional Lyrics

2. How many years can a mountain exist
   Before it's washed to the sea?
   How many years can some people exist
   Before they're allowed to be free?
   How many times can a man turn his head,
   And pretend that he just doesn't see?

3. How many times must a man look up
   Before he can see the sky?
   How many ears must one man have
   Before he can hear people cry?
   How many deaths will it take till he knows
   That too many people have died?

Behind Blue Eyes

Words and Music by Pete Townshend

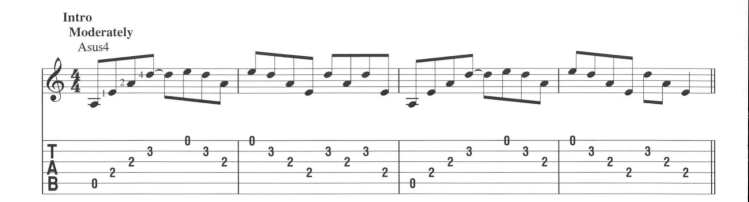

Intro
Moderately
Asus4

Verse
Am   C   G

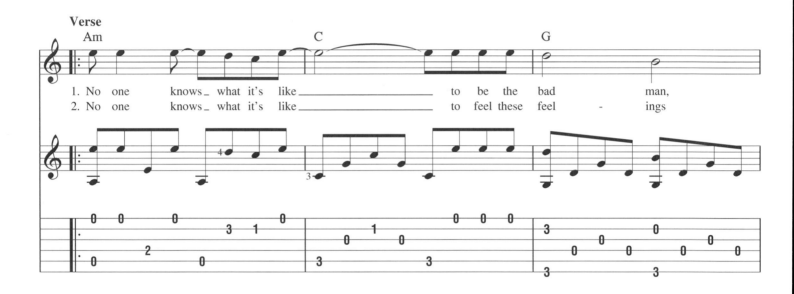

1. No one   knows_ what it's like _____ to be the bad   man,
2. No one   knows_ what it's like _____ to feel these feel - ings

F

to be the sad   man   be -
like I ___ do, _____   and

Copyright © 1971 by Towser Tunes, Inc., ABKCO Music and Fabulous Music Ltd.
Copyright Renewed
All Rights for Towser Tunes, Inc. Administered by BMG Music Publishing International
All Rights for BMG Music Publishing International in the U.S. Administered by Careers-BMG Music Publishing, Inc.
International Copyright Secured All Rights Reserved

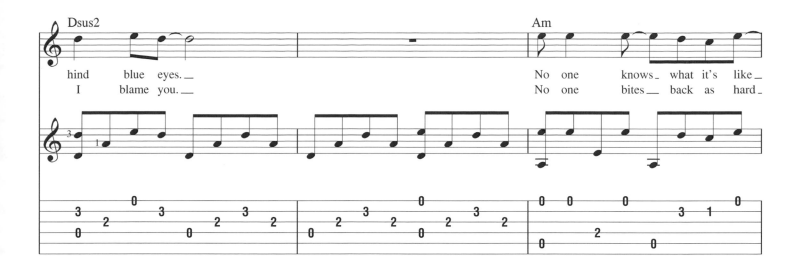

hind blue eyes. ___
I blame you. ___

No one knows ___ what it's like ___
No one bites ___ back as hard ___

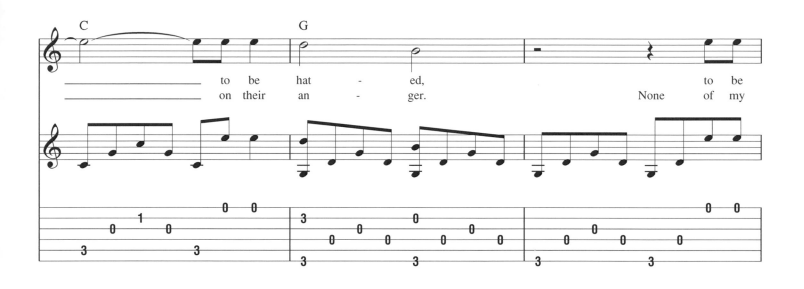

___ to be hat - ed,
___ on their an - ger.

to be
None of my

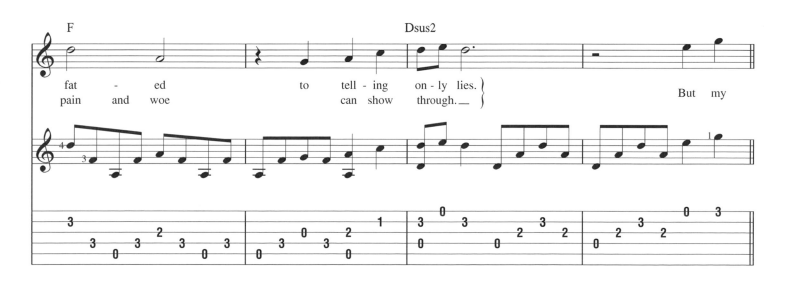

fat - ed
pain and woe

to tell - ing on - ly lies.
can show through. ___

But my

Chorus

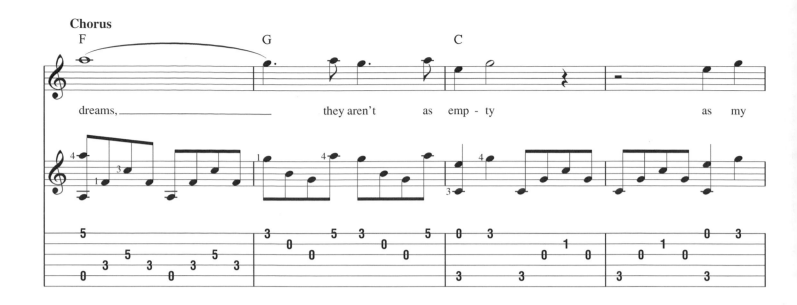

dreams,_____ they aren't as emp - ty as my

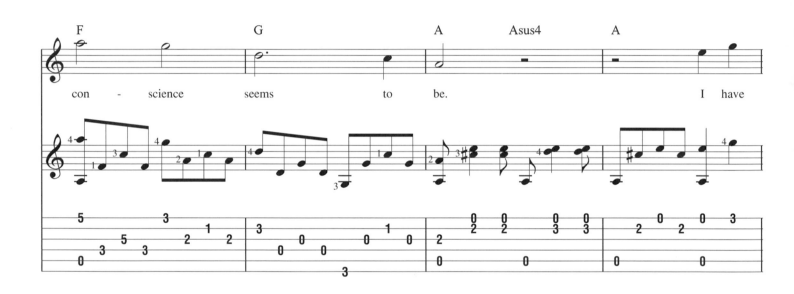

con - science seems to be. I have

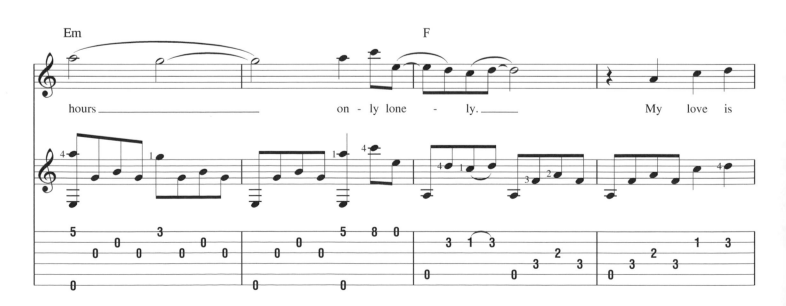

hours_____ on - ly lone - ly._____ My love is

ven - gence   that's nev - er free.

3. When my fist clench - es, crack it o - pen_____ be - fore I use_____

Best of My Love

Words and Music by John David Souther, Don Henley and Glenn Frey

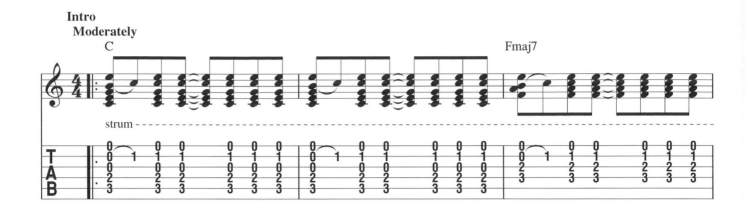

© 1974 (Renewed 2002) EMI BLACKWOOD MUSIC INC., CASS COUNTY MUSIC and RED CLOUD MUSIC
All Rights Reserved   International Copyright Secured   Used by Permission

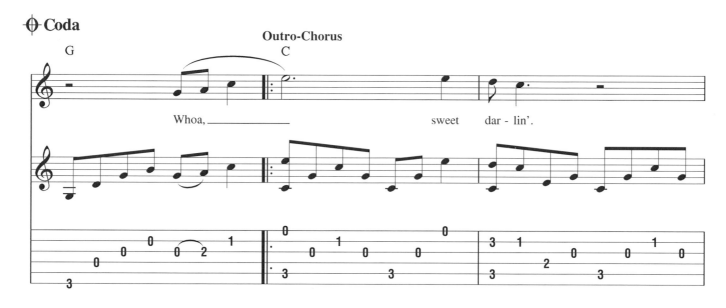

Additional Lyrics

2. Beautiful faces and loud empty places, look at the way we live.
Wastin' our time on cheap talk and wine, left us so little to give.
That same old crowd was like a cold, dark cloud that we could never rise above.
But here in my heart, I give you the best of my love.

3. But ev'ry morning I wake up and worry what's gonna happen today.
You see it your way and I see it mine but we both see it slippin' away.
You know we always had each other, baby. I guess it wasn't enough.
Oh, oh, but here in my heart, I give you the best of my love.

The Boxer

Words and Music by Paul Simon

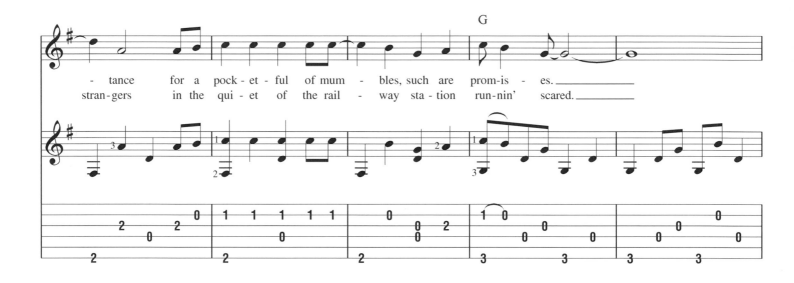

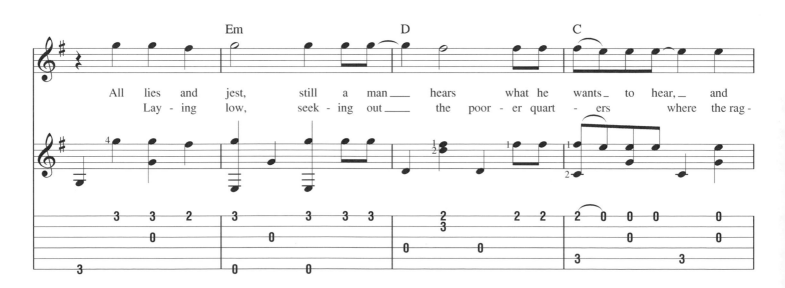

Copyright © 1968 (Renewed) Paul Simon Music (BMI)
International Copyright Secured   All Rights Reserved
Reprinted by Permission of Music Sales Corporation

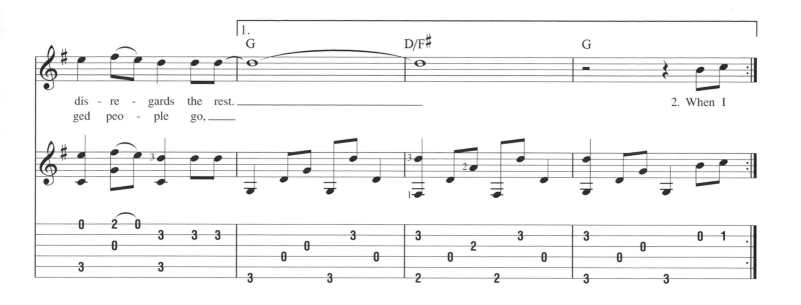

dis - re - gards the rest._____
ged peo - ple go, _____

2. When I

_____ look - in' for the plac - es on - ly they would know.

𝄋 Chorus

Lie, la, lie. Lie, la, lie, la, lie, la,

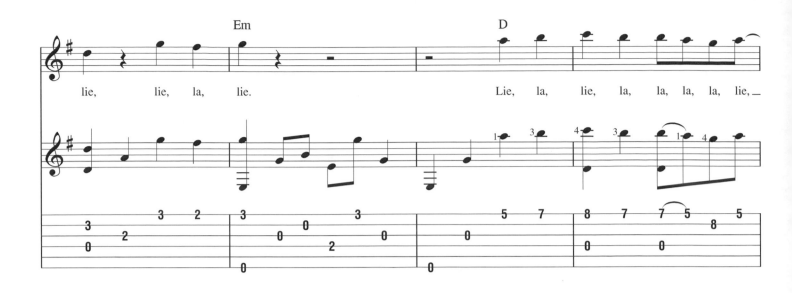

lie,   lie,   la,   lie.   Lie,   la,   lie,   la,   la,   la,   la,   lie,

_____   la,   la,   la,   la,   lie. _____   3. Ask - ing on -

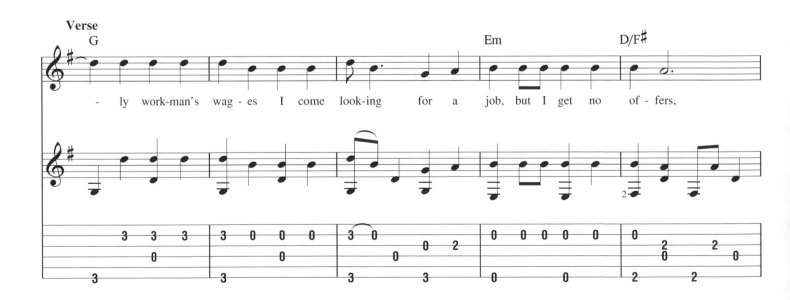

- ly   work-man's   wag - es   I   come   look-ing   for   a   job,   but   I   get   no   of - fers,

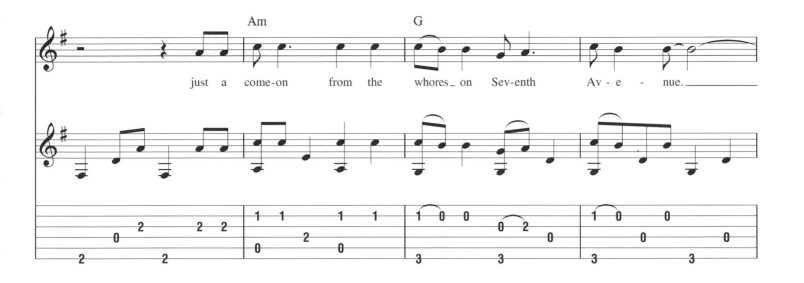

just a come-on from the whores on Sev-enth Av - e - nue.

I do de - clare, there were times when I was so lone-some I

took some com - fort there. La, la, la, la, la, la, la.

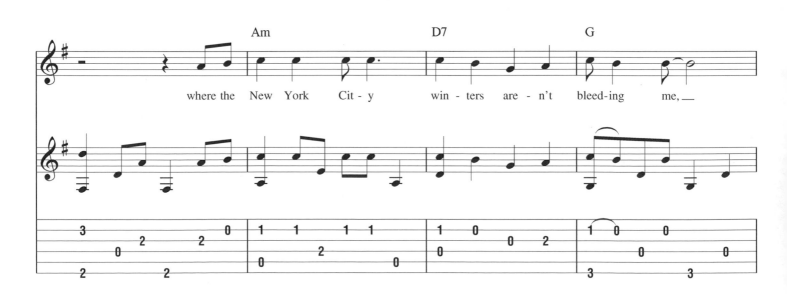

Outro-Chorus

an - ger and his shame. I am leav - ing, I am leav - ing but the fight - er still re -

mains. Lie, la, lie. Lie, la, lie, la, lie, la,

lie, lie, la, lie. Lie, la, lie, la, la, la, la, lie, _

_ la, la, la, la, lie. Lie, la,

In My Life

Words and Music by John Lennon and Paul McCartney

Copyright © 1965 Sony/ATV Songs LLC
Copyright Renewed
All Rights Administered by Sony/ATV Music Publishing, 8 Music Square West, Nashville, TN 37203
International Copyright Secured   All Rights Reserved

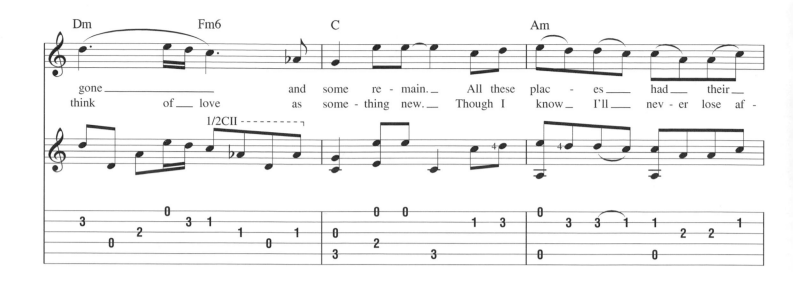

gone _____ and some re - main. _ All these plac - es _____ had _____ their _____

think of _____ love as some - thing new. _ Though I know _____ I'll _____ nev - er lose af -

mo - ments with lov - ers and friends _____ I still can re - call. _____ Some are

fec - tion for peo - ple and things _____ that went be - fore. _____ I

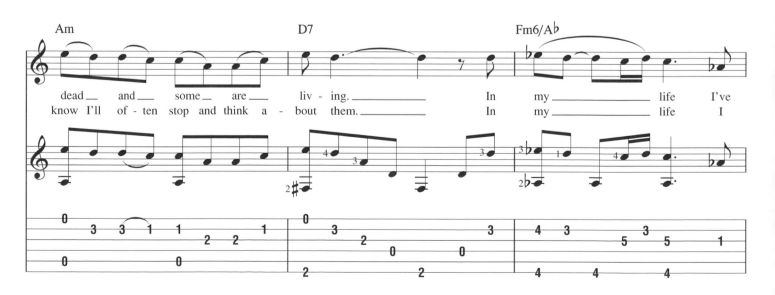

dead _____ and _____ some _____ are _____ liv - ing. _____ In my _____ life I've

know I'll of - ten stop and think a - bout them. _____ In my _____ life I

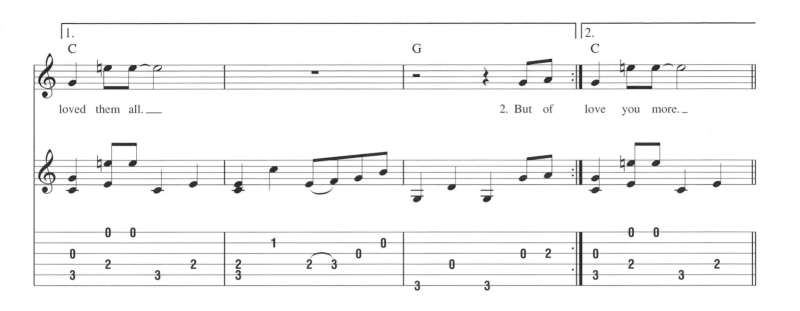

loved them all. ___

2. But of love you more. _

Outro

Slowly

In my ___ life I

A tempo

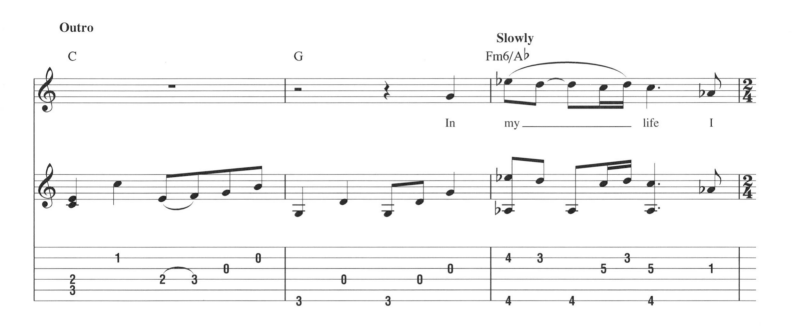

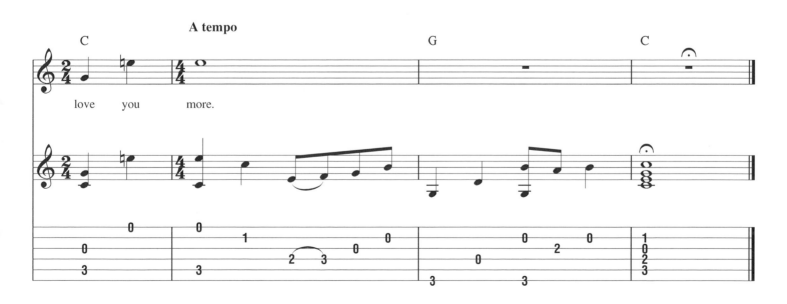

love you more.

Dust in the Wind

Words and Music by Kerry Livgren

© 1977, 1978 EMI BLACKWOOD MUSIC INC. and DON KIRSHNER MUSIC
All Rights Controlled and Administered by EMI BLACKWOOD MUSIC INC.
All Rights Reserved   International Copyright Secured   Used by Permission

on - ly for a mo - ment, and the mo-ment's gone._____ All

my dreams_____ pass be - fore my eyes a cu - ri -

os - i - ty._____ Dust in the wind._____

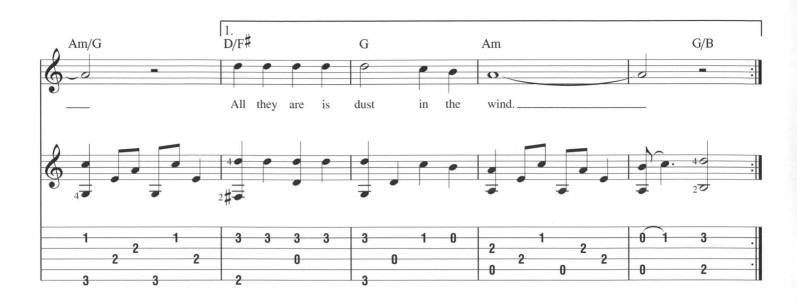

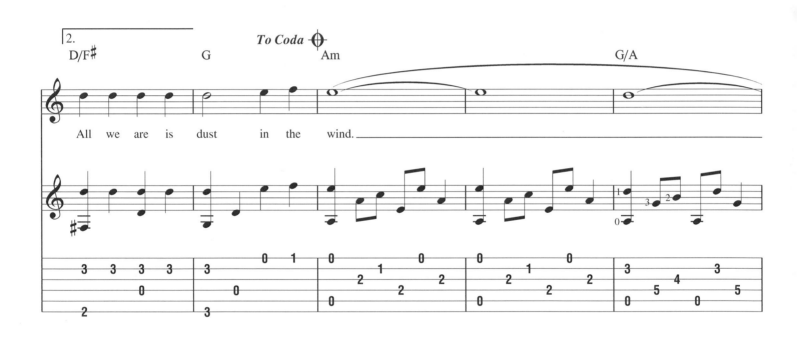

Additional Lyrics

2. Same old song,
   Just a drop of water in an endless sea.
   All we do
   Crumbles to the ground though we refuse to see.

3. Now, don't hang on,
   Nothing lasts forever but the earth and sky.
   It slips away,
   And all your money won't another minute buy.

Helplessly Hoping

Words and Music by Stephen Stills

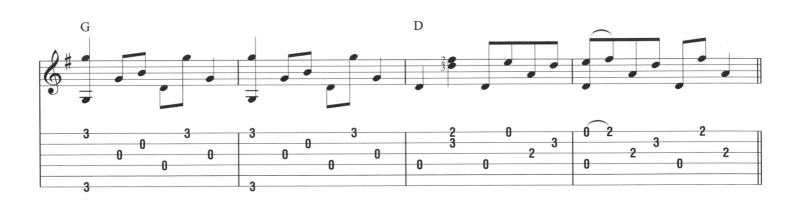

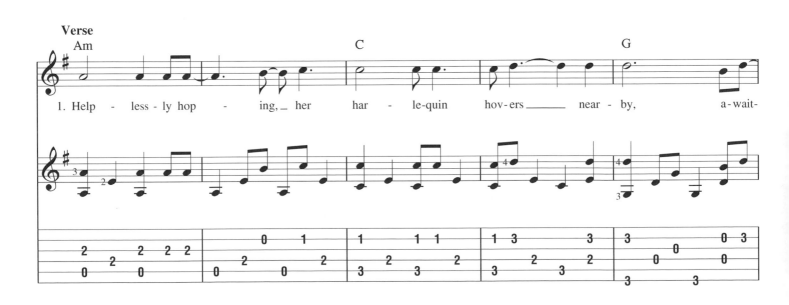

Copyright © 1969 Gold Hill Music Inc.
Copyright Renewed
All Rights Administered by Sony/ATV Music Publishing, 8 Music Square West, Nashville, TN 37203
International Copyright Secured   All Rights Reserved

win - dow_ and won-ders at the emp - ty place_ in - side.
cer - tain_ to tell you con-fu - sion has_ its cost.

Heart - less-ly help - ing_ him - self to her bad dreams,_ he wor-ries, did he_
Love is - n't ly - ing,_ it's loose in a la - dy____ who lin-gers,

____ hear a good - bye, or e - ven_____ hel - lo?
say she is lost and chok - ing_____ on hel - lo._

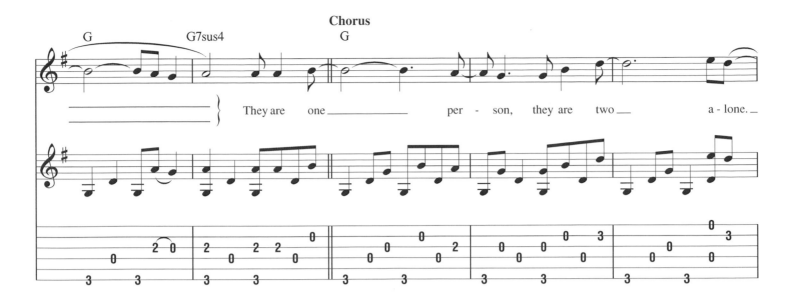

They are one _____ per - son, they are two ___ a - lone. _

_____ They are three ___ to-geth - er, they are for _____ each

oth - er.

Hey Jude

Words and Music by John Lennon and Paul McCartney

Copyright © 1968 Sony/ATV Songs LLC
Copyright Renewed
All Rights Administered by Sony/ATV Music Publishing, 8 Music Square West, Nashville, TN 37203
International Copyright Secured   All Rights Reserved

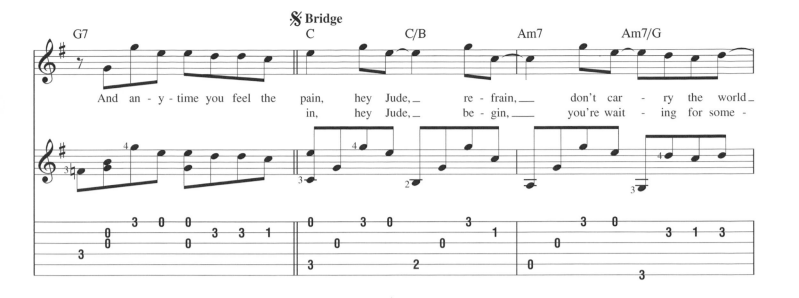

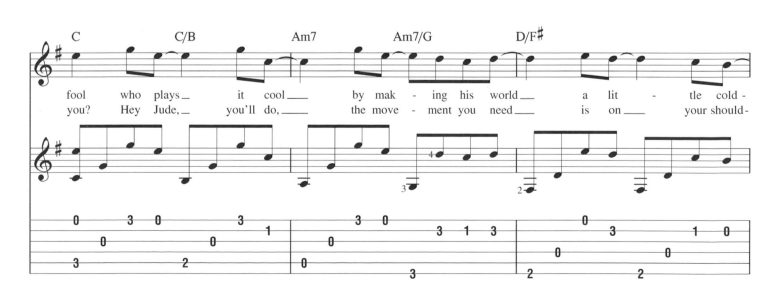

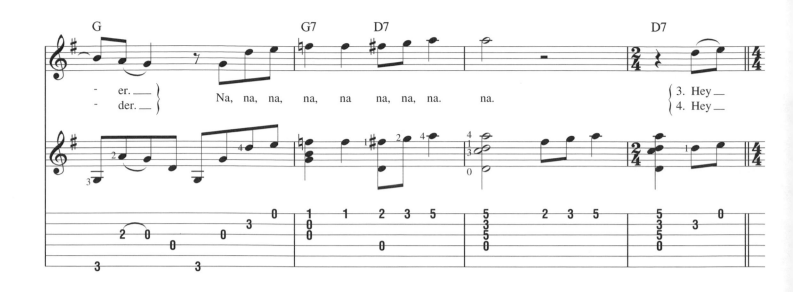

36

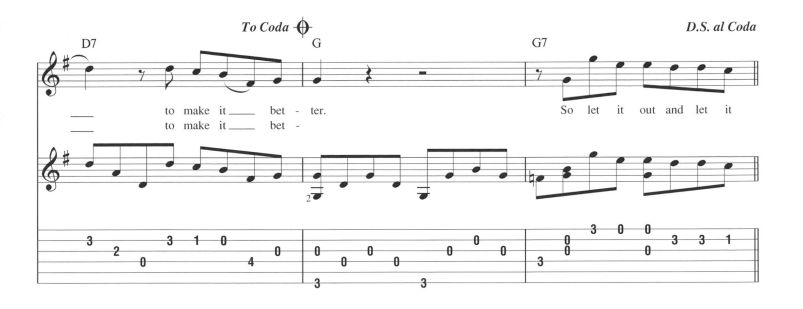

Learning to Fly

Words and Music by Jeff Lynne and Tom Petty

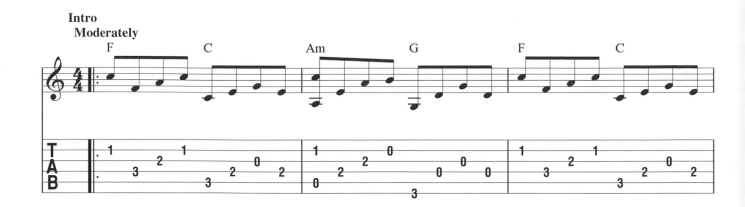

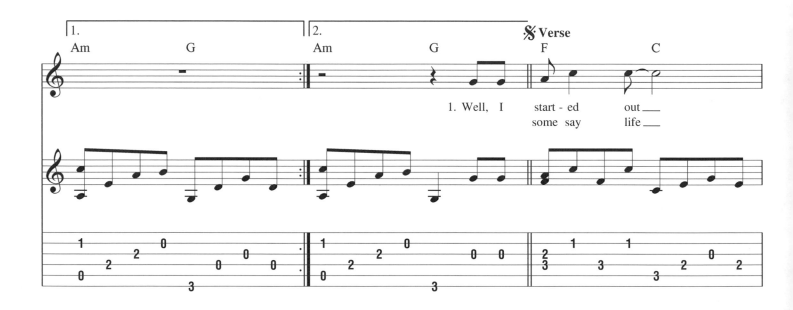

1. Well, I start-ed out___
   some say life___

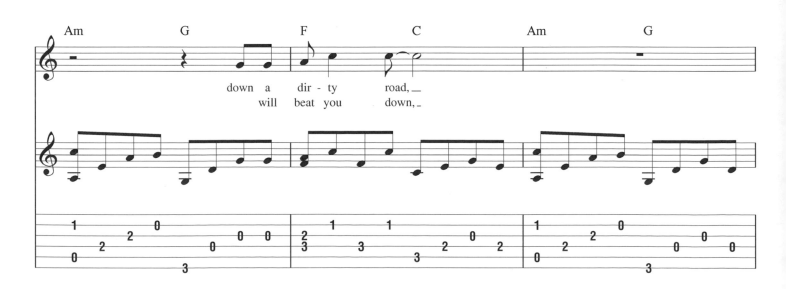

down a dir-ty road,___
will beat you down,___

(c) 1991 EMI APRIL MUSIC INC. and GONE GATOR MUSIC
All Rights Reserved   International Copyright Secured   Used by Permission

start - ed out ___ all a - lone. ___
break your heart, ___ steal your crown. ___

Verse

2. And the sun went down ___ as I
good old days ___ may
5. So I start - ed out ___ for

crossed the hill ___ and the town lit up, ___
not re - turn, ___ and the rocks might melt, ___
God knows where. ___ I guess I'll know ___

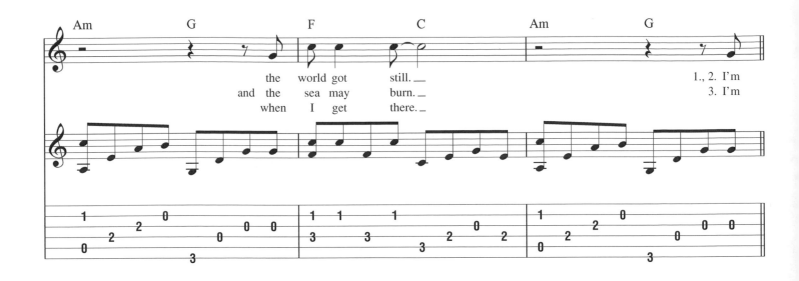

Chorus

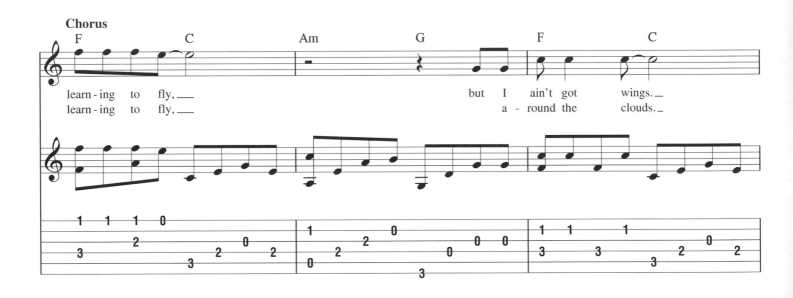

Interlude

Coda

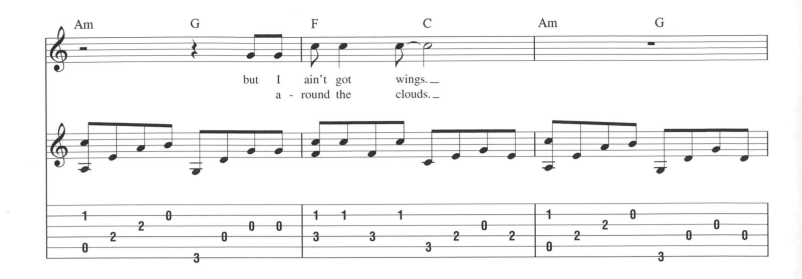

but I ain't got wings.
a - round the clouds.

Com - ing down
What goes up
Learn - ing to fly.

is the hard - est thing.
must come down.

1., 2.

I'm
I'm

3.

Leaving on a Jet Plane

Words and Music by John Denver

Copyright © 1967 Cherry Lane Music Publishing Company, Inc. (ASCAP) and DreamWorks Songs (ASCAP)
Rights for DreamWorks Songs Administered by Cherry Lane Music Publishing Company, Inc.
International Copyright Secured   All Rights Reserved

Additional Lyrics

2. There's so many times I've let you down,
   So many times I've played around.
   I tell you now, they don't mean a thing.
   Ev'ry place I go, I'll think of you,
   Ev'ry song I sing, I'll sing for you.
   When I come back, I'll wear your wedding ring.

3. Now the time has come to leave you,
   One more time let me kiss you.
   Then close your eyes, I'll be on my way.
   Dream about the days to come,
   When I won't have to leave alone,
   About the times I won't have to say...

Patience

Words and Music by W. Axl Rose, Slash, Izzy Stradlin', Duff McKagan and Steven Adler

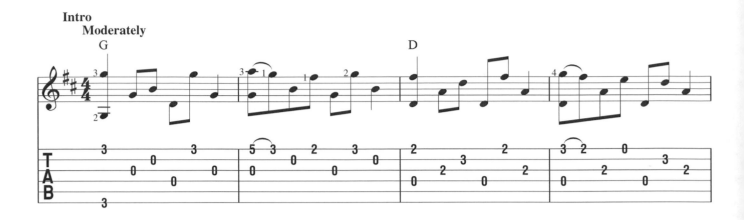

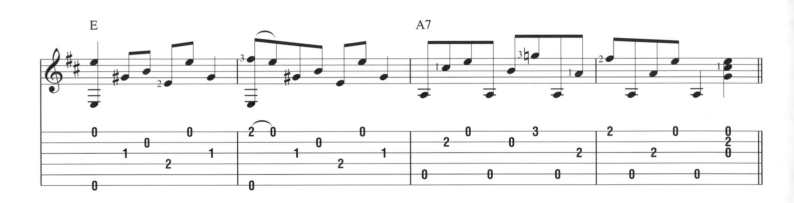

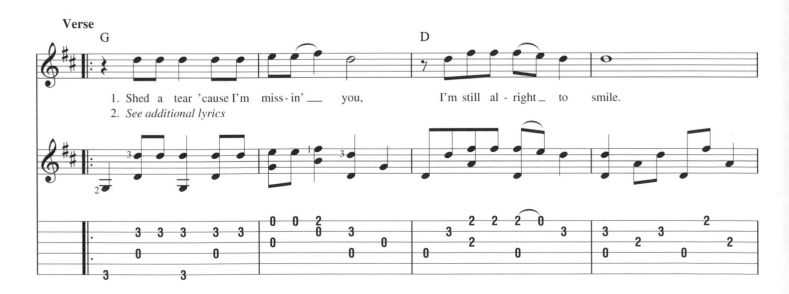

1. Shed a tear 'cause I'm miss-in' ___ you,   I'm still al - right ___ to smile.

2. *See additional lyrics*

Copyright © 1988 Guns N' Roses Music (ASCAP)
International Copyright Secured   All Rights Reserved

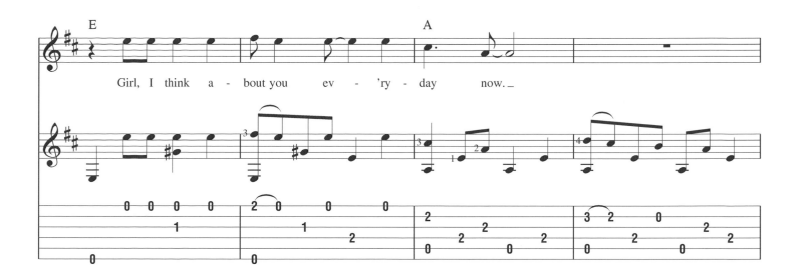

Girl, I think a - bout you ev - 'ry - day now.

Was a time when I was - n't___ sure but you set my mind___ at ease.

There is no doubt you're in___ my heart now.

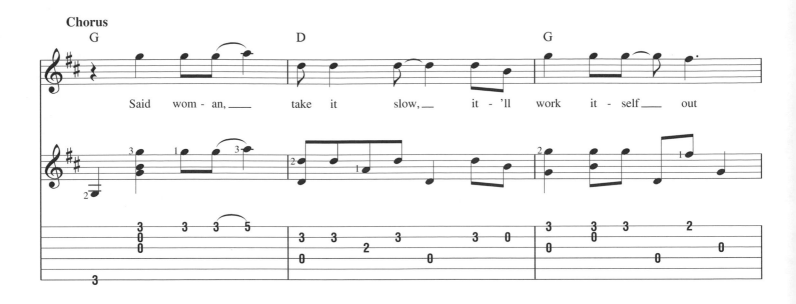

Said wom-an,___ take it slow,___ it-'ll work it-self ___ out

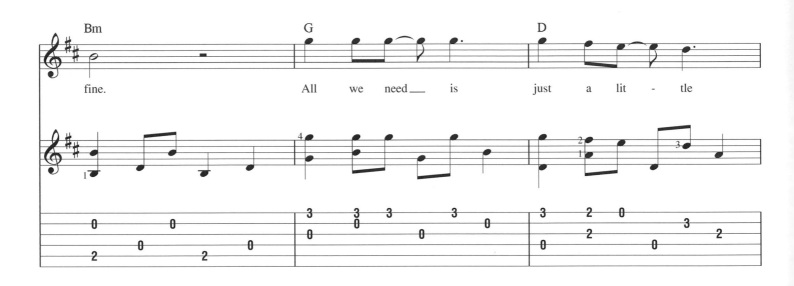

fine.   All we need___ is   just a lit-tle

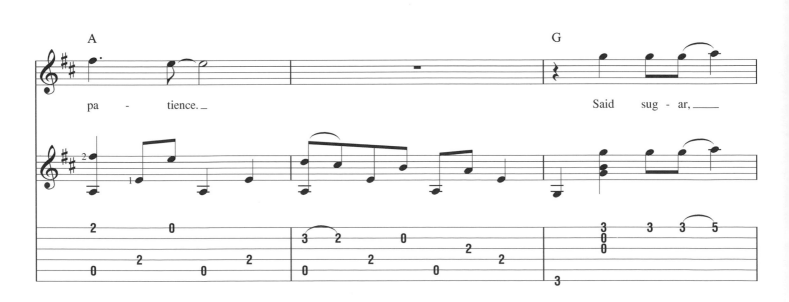

pa - tience. ___   Said sug-ar,___

make it   slow ___   and we come to - geth - er   fine.

All   we need ___ is   just a lit - tle   pa - tience. ___

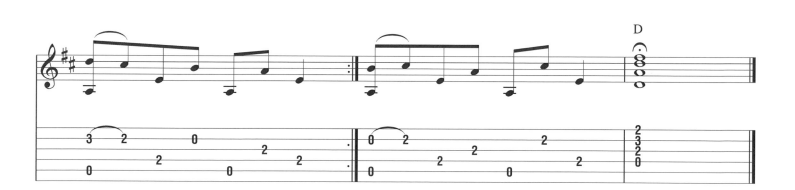

Additional Lyrics

2. I sit here on the stairs 'cause I'd rather be alone.
   If I can't have you right now I'll wait, dear.
   Sometimes I get so tense but I can't speed up the time.
   But you know, love, there's one more thing to consider.

Tears in Heaven

Words and Music by Eric Clapton and Will Jennings

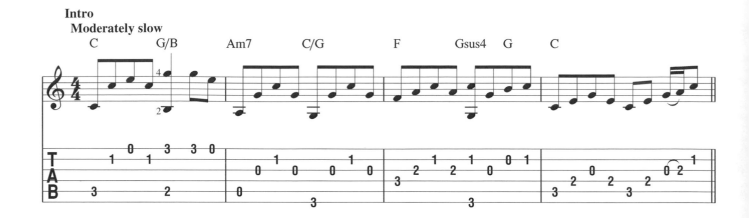

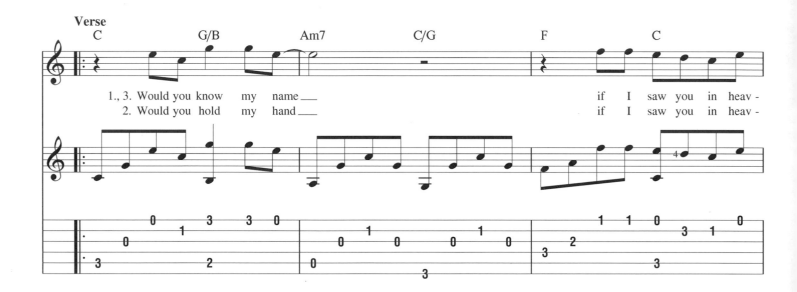

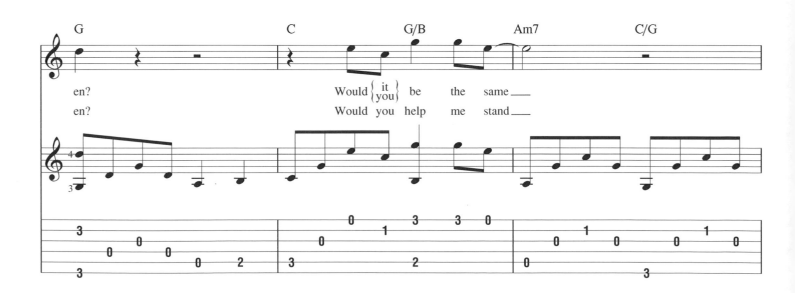

Copyright © 1992 by E.C. Music Ltd. and Blue Sky Rider Songs
All Rights for E.C. Music Ltd. Administered by Unichappell Music Inc.
All Rights for Blue Sky Rider Songs Administered by Irving Music, Inc.
International Copyright Secured   All Rights Reserved

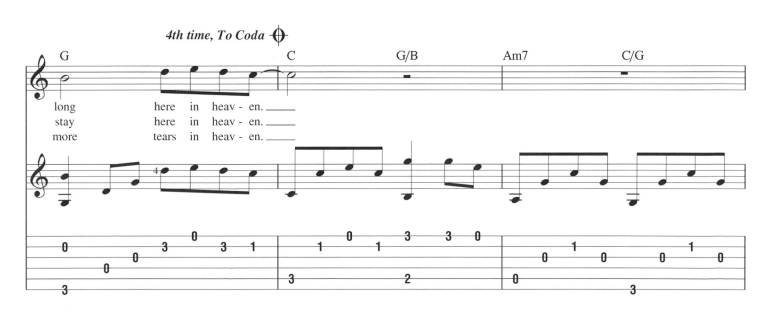

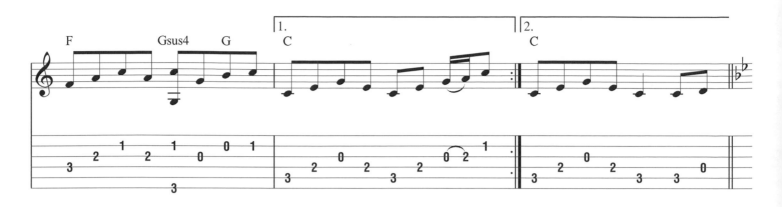

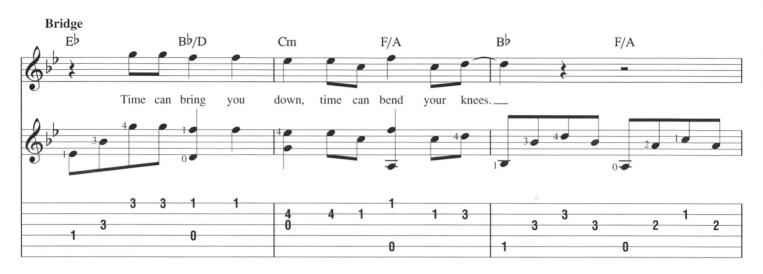

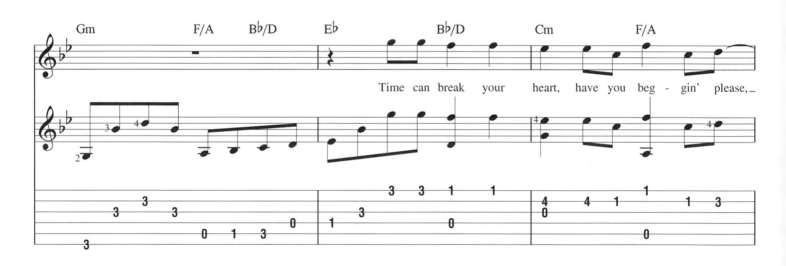

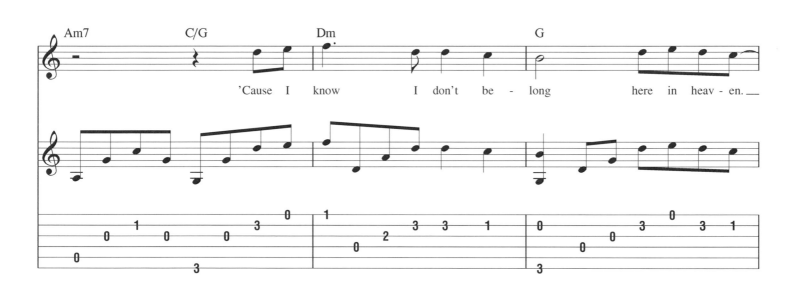

'Cause I know   I don't be - long   here in heav - en. __

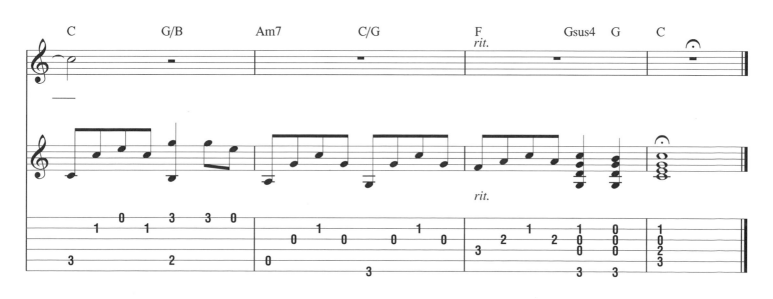

This Land Is Your Land

Words and Music by Woody Guthrie

Verse

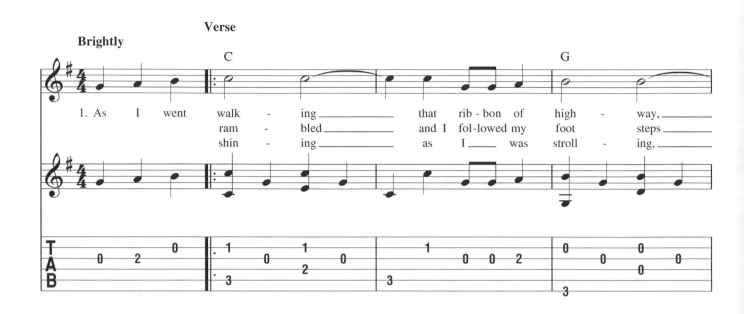

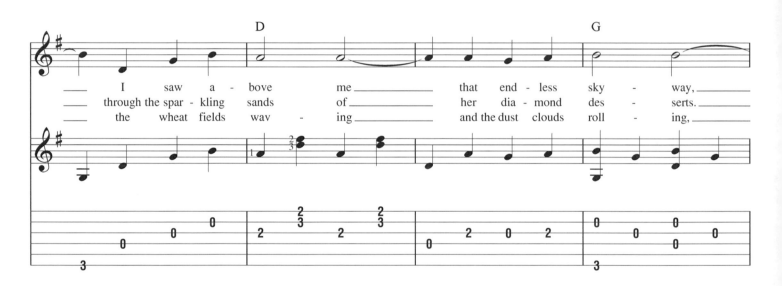

TRO - © Copyright 1956 (Renewed), 1958 (Renewed), 1970 (Renewed) and 1972 (Renewed) Ludlow Music, Inc., New York, NY
International Copyright Secured
All Rights Reserved Including Public Performance For Profit
Used by Permission

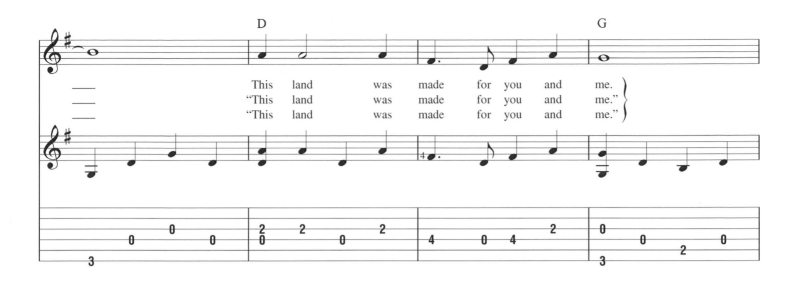

This land was made for you and me.
"This land was made for you and me."
"This land was made for you and me."

Chorus

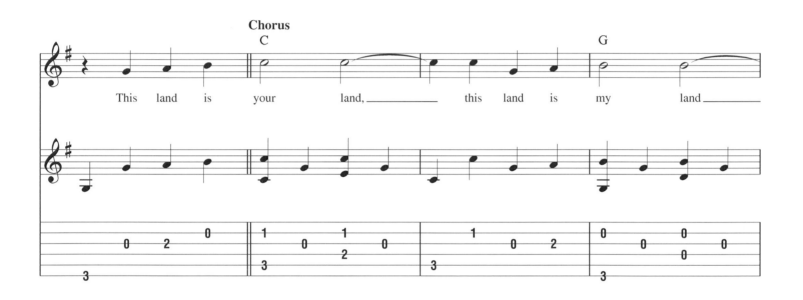

This land is your land, _____ this land is my land _____

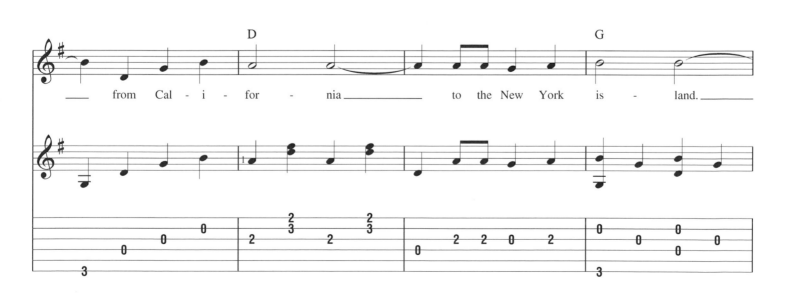

_____ from Cal - i - for - nia _____ to the New York is - land. _____

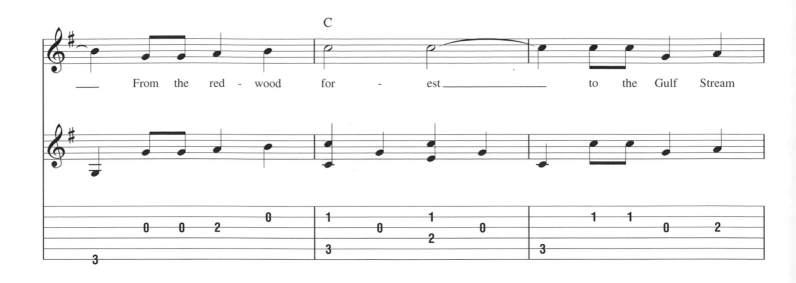

From the red - wood for - est_____ to the Gulf Stream

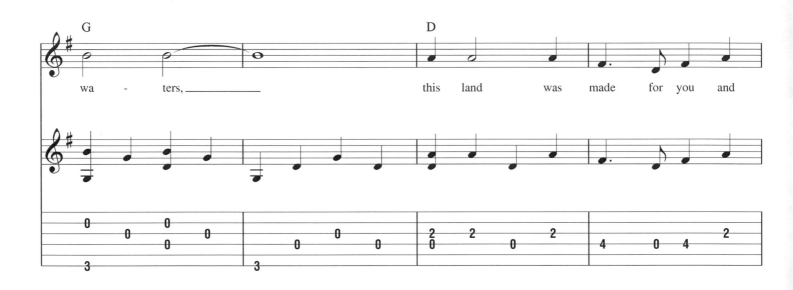

wa - ters,_____ this land was made for you and

me._____ 2. I've roamed and me._____
3. Well, the sun came

Time in a Bottle

Words and Music by Jim Croce

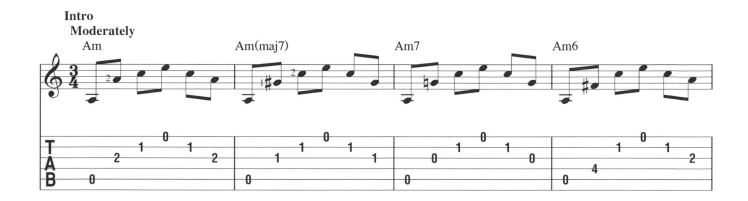

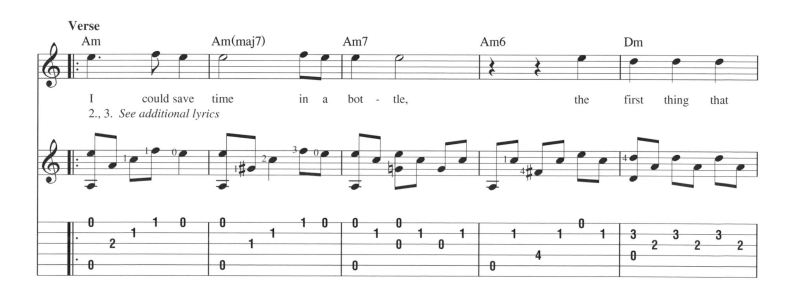

Copyright © 1971 (Renewed) Time In A Bottle and Croce Publishing (ASCAP)
All Rights Reserved   Used by Permission

You've Got a Friend

Words and Music by Carole King

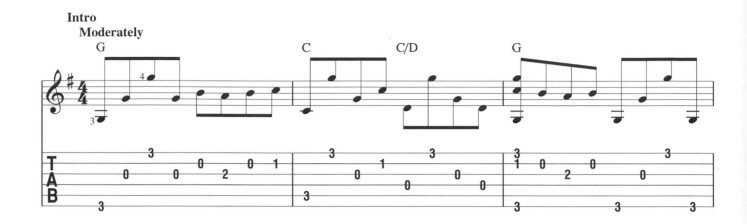

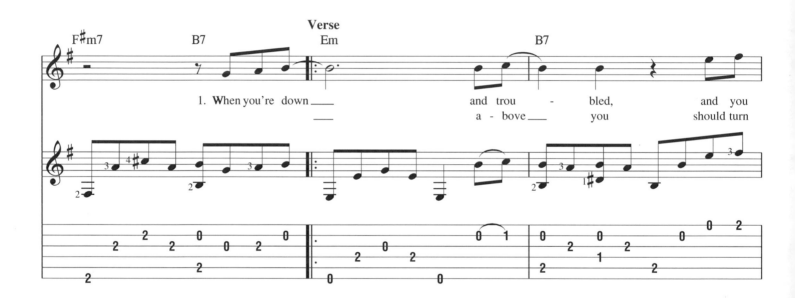

© 1971 (Renewed 1999) COLGEMS-EMI MUSIC INC.
All Rights Reserved   International Copyright Secured   Used by Permission

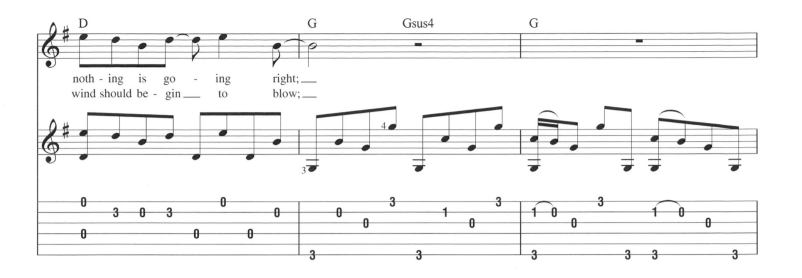

noth - ing is go - ing right; ___
wind should be - gin ___ to blow; ___

close your eyes ___ and think of me, ___ and soon I will be
keep you head ___ to - geth - er and call my name out

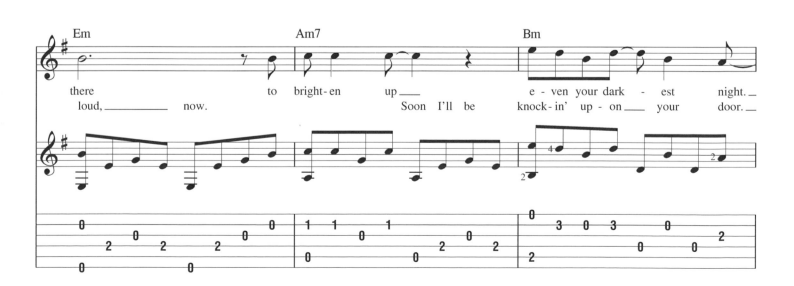

there to bright- en up ___ e - ven your dark - est night. ___
loud, _____ now. Soon I'll be knock- in' up - on ___ your door. ___